Colourful
New Zealand

Text by
Sally Nicholson

Photographs by
Warren Jacobs

Kowhai

INTRODUCTION

New Zealand can in many ways be thankful for its isolated situation in the southwest corner of the Pacific Ocean. It lies between the southern latitudes 37° to 43° with its nearest neighbour being Australia 2,000 kilometres to the northwest, while to the east the whole Pacific Ocean separates it from the continent of South America.

The late arrival of man to these southern islands is not surprising when you consider the distances required to travel through notoriously treacherous seas. Polynesian navigators in primitive outrigger canoes reached New Zealand's shores only a thousand years ago, an amazing feat by these ancestors of our Maori race. The first European settlers arrived much later at the turn of the 19th Century, so New Zealand is young for a developed country. Today's multi-racial society strives to protect its natural environment. It can boast of room for individuals to grow in a country free from extremes of climate, famine, or fear of hostile neighbours.

Climate plays an important role in New Zealand's good fortune. The narrow group of islands, no part being wider than 240 kilometres has a good balance of sunshine and rain, perfect conditions for the growth of good pasture often so green and velvet-like in certain areas it resembles a well cared for golf course. New Zealand's wind and rain patterns are influenced by its mountain ranges, particularly in the South Island where the Southern Alps form a barrier causing moisture bearing clouds from the Tasman Sea to distribute their rain predominantly onto the West Coast. However there is enough precipitation on the east coast to ensure a high yield of sheep and dairy products and ample foodstuffs for New Zealand's 3.2 million people.

Britain was once the major buyer of New Zealand's primary products but the protectionism of the European Common Market has forced her to look to new markets e.g. Asia and the Middle East. Diversification and changes in presentation were necessary. Great interest developed in the farming of

Left

It is hard to imagine these peaceful waters of Mangonui as once being a busy port where locally felled kauri trees were floated ashore to be milled and exported by the waiting overseas ships to European markets. Today the subtropical climate and excellent fishing make Mangonui an attractive resort for many North Islanders.

deer, not so long ago considered an uncontrollable pest causing erosion in our high country and native bush. An even more recent change has been Angora goat farming, where astronomical prices are being paid for prized stud animals. Along with this is continued progress in establishing new and more economical methods of cropping and a stimulated fishing industry. Steps have been taken to promote the growth of tourism and industry to safeguard New Zealand from being totally reliant on agriculture for its income.

But for most visitors to "Aotearoa" (New Zealand's Maori name meaning "land of the long white cloud") it is the sheer beauty and contrast of the landscape that provides the most impact. It could be the massive peaks of the Southern Alps or the cone shaped volcanoes of the north, the fiords and glaciers of southern Westland or the enormity of trout filled Lake Taupo in the North Island's central plateau, the crispness of early winter skiing on any of the numerous fields of the South Island or the bubbling mudpools and steaming geysers of Rotorua's thermal region. Everywhere it seems are large sparsely populated areas where New Zealanders and visitors alike can indulge in both summer and winter outdoor activities, so much a part of the New Zealand way of life. It is a common scene to see groups with tents and packs retreating to mountains, lakes, rivers or beaches which are never far from anyone's backdoor.

The heritage of New Zealand's remoteness has had an influence on the character of its people. Adaptability and ingenuity, qualities so necessary for survival in the early colonial days are still evident in the New Zealanders of the 20th Century. They are a happy marriage of friendliness and an ability to get onto the task in hand. Opportunities are available for those who strive for success. There are the rich and the poor but the disparity between the two groups is much less pronounced than in other countries, the majority falling somewhere in the middle. When taking all things into consideration, New Zealanders are indeed fortunate in the beauty of their environment and the quality of life it offers to them.

Page 1 Styx Jail, Paerua

Page 2–3 Lake Hawea

THE NORTH ISLAND

To be able to differentiate clearly the physical features of the North Island to that of the South, it is an advantage to become airborne. It is from the air that one can quite distinctly see evidence of the fault line from which New Zealand erupted above sea level many centuries ago and which had such an effect on the geography of the North Island. Begin your flight over the smoking volcanic peak of White Island in the Bay of Plenty. Fly south over the steaming lakes and geysers of Rotorua to New Zealand's largest lake, Lake Taupo, formed by the subsidence of very early geothermal activity. Follow the chain of still active volcanoes of the central plateau, Ruapehu, Ngauruhoe and Tongariro, casting a look right if it's a clear day to the distinctive cone of Mt Taranaki and you can see what is unique about the North Island of New Zealand.

It shares the reputation, along with Iceland and Yellowstone Park, U.S.A. of being one of the main geothermal areas of the world. Throughout the North Island's central plateau the earth's crust is so thin that energy built up beneath the surface forces its way through any available crack or fault, often in the form of shooting geysers sending jets of scalding water high into the air. There are "hot lakes" large and small with Waimangu's crater having the distinction of being the world's largest volume of natural boiling water. Many of these pools have colourful silicon terraces whose iridescent hues are dependent on the variety of minerals present in the water. It is even possible to hook one of Taupo's famous trout from a stream and cook it in a neighbouring boiling pool.

The North Island has many other interesting features as well as its geothermal region. The subtropical and popular big game fishing areas of the Bay of Islands and the far north were the very centre of New Zealand's early history and for that alone are fascinating. In those days vast forests of New Zealand's giant tree, the kauri, covered this region. Today visitors can

Left

It was here on the peaceful waters of Lake Tarawera that on 31st May 1886 a phantom war canoe was seen speeding across the lake. The local Maori people of the time thought it to be an omen of disaster. Only 11 days later, on June 10th, the northern peak of Mt Tarawera erupted and the chain of explosions that followed caused loss of life and devastation over an area of 16,000 sq km. The world famous pink and white silica terraces on the shores of Lake Rotomahana were totally destroyed.

only reminisce on what must have been before the mass cutting of these tall thick trunks of straightgrained timber, firstly for early settlers' homes and then for export, as they were highly sought after as masts and spars for the British Navy's fleet. A few remaining stands of these "kings of the forest" can be found at Waipoua or Trounson Kauri Park where they are rigidly protected.

Travelling south to Auckland and through to the Waikato Valley and Taranaki are vast areas of easy rolling green hills where many of New Zealand's best dairy herds are to be found, whilst in the lush grasslands of Hawke's Bay and undulating hills of the King Country sheep and fat lambs thrive. Water is plentiful, nowhere more so than in the largest river of New Zealand, the Waikato, which has numerous hydro electric schemes all feeding valuable power into the national grid.

When describing the coastlines of the North Island it is difficult not to repeat oneself and talk of the various bays, inlets and sweeping beaches from Cape Reinga to the Wellington Harbour as being favourite holiday spots, as they all are. All share the role as sites for a very important part of New Zealand life, the holiday home. Sometimes a small unpretentious weatherboard cottage and sometimes a palatial architecturally designed mansion fit for any Home and Garden magazine, baches, as they are called in the north, are scattered along both eastern and western coastlines. In the summer holidaymakers are everywhere, boating, fishing and swimming, or just lazing on the beach with a book and a can of beer.

A wellknown T.V. personality now actively involved in promoting her city says "Auckland is a burgeoning sophisticate, if a little plastic". With a population of 880,000 New Zealand's largest city, situated on an 8 km isthmus dividing the Tasman Sea and Pacific Ocean is home to more people than are to be found in the whole of the South Island. Reminiscent of Sydney with its many fine beaches, sailing on the Waitemata Harbour and an impressive bridge connecting downtown Auckland to its sprawling satellite cities, Auckland is certainly on the move. It also bears the title "Capital of Polynesia" with more Pacific Islanders living here than anywhere in the world, making Auckland a truly multiracial city.

Wellington, the seat of government and capital of New Zealand could never be called "plastic". It is condensed into the foreshore of a magnificent natural harbour. Architecturally exciting much use has been made of reclaimed land and shelved hillsites with spectacular views over the everchanging skyline of the city's commercial area. Here are to be found the government department head offices and those of many of the country's important companies. It may be significant that a very recent Mall was built underground — perhaps Wellingtonians are finally accepting their title of "Windy Wellington".

Comparing the North Island to the South, one of the greatest differences is in its people. The North Island is the centre of Maoridom, 93% of all Maori people reside here. Queen Te Ata-i-rangi-kaahu, the present leader of the Maori people lives in Ngaruawahia and throughout the island, particularly in the rural areas of the far north and East Cape groups of Maori are living in their traditional extended family where caring and sharing, ideals often lost in Pakeha society, are of great importance. Rotorua is where the tourist may experience many of the cultural activities of the Maori people. Greater awareness and emphasis is being felt throughout the country on the making of a better Maori and Pakeha society, evidence of which is seen in the increasing use of both languages and philosophies in the life of New Zealand people of the 1980s.

Below

Opua Bay provides a car ferry service for those travelling from Paihia to the historic township of Russell. Though only 7 km apart, the road distance without the ferry would be 109 km. East of Opua lies the historic pa site of Chief Pomare II which was razed to the ground in 1845 by the British because of Pomare's suspected collaboration with the infamous Hone Heke.

Right

Waipoua Kauri Forest, northwest of Dargaville is the last significant stand of native kauri in New Zealand. Before the exploitation of the timber by the early settlers, giant trees such as this covered most of Northland Peninsula and down to the south of Auckland. Te Matua Ngahere, translated "King of the Forest" is possibly 2,000 years old with a girth of 16.1 metres and a height of 30 metres. Waipoua's remaining 2,500 hectares of indigenous trees were declared a forest sanctuary in 1952.

Below

Cape Reinga is commonly thought the most northern point in New Zealand, where Tasman and Pacific waters meet. Surville Cliffs are actually 4.8 km further north but easier access to Reinga along Ninety Mile Beach make it the more popular spot to view the very top of New Zealand. An ancient Pohutukawa tree below the lighthouse adds to this claim, as it is here the spirits of the Maori departed are said to rest before their final journey back to their homeland of "Hawaiki".

Waitangi has other claims apart from being the historic reserve where New Zealand's nationhood began with the signing of the somewhat controversial Treaty between Maori and Pakeha. It has hospitable beaches, an interesting shipboard museum at the Waitangi Bridge and ferry services across to Russell or Round-the-Bays.

Wainui Bay is one of the splendid beaches east of the Whangaroa Harbour. Its golden sands and Pohutukawa studded grassy headland is relatively peaceful at peak holiday times because of the more difficult road access here than to a lot of the more heavily frequented beaches of Northland.

Right

When the site of the signing of the Treaty of Waitangi and the former dwelling of James Bushby came up for sale in 1931, the then Governor General and his wife Lord and Lady Bledisloe generously purchased it for the nation and set up a Trust Board of suitable Maori and Pakeha dignitaries to administer the property. Along with the magnificent Whare Runanga the Maori people built this great Waitangi Canoe as their contribution. The canoe is used on special occasions with all the ceremony of days of old.

Below

The traditional dress of a Maori maiden is a bodice of handtwisted tanika work, a piu piu or skirt made from scraped, dyed and rolled flax leaves and a handcarved pendant, often the hei-tiki made of greenstone, the native translucent nephrite. The poi hanging from her waist she skilfully twirls while singing traditional poi songs.

Left

Kawau Bay is a favourite yachtsman's haven. Sandspit, a small wharf in the bay, is the ferry terminal for the popular trip across to Kawau Island, once the property of an early New Zealand Governor and Prime Minister, Sir George Grey. Grey's Mansion House (c. 1862) has been faithfully restored by the Historic Places Trust.

Below

Tree ferns are perhaps the most distinctive feature of the New Zealand forest, especially in areas where they can obtain plenty of light to regenerate. There are six species known as tree ferns, all usually single trunked with a huge crown of majestic fronds.

Bottom

The rather sophisticated cousin of the unpopular hillside scrub broom, the Kowhai is a legume, growing usually at the edge of the forest. It starts its life as a spindly shrub but given the protection of the forest canopy can grow into a sizable tree, showing a great cluster of yellow flowers in the spring.

Far right

Auckland city is built on the narrow Tamaki Peninsula, with Manukau Harbour to one side and Waitemata Harbour to the other. A sprawling city larger than Greater London in area and similar to Sydney in style, it is the largest of New Zealand's cities. It is often referred to as the capital of Polynesia, having more Pacific Islanders than any other centre.

Right

Parnell Village, not so long ago a run down inner Auckland suburb, won a national tourist award when restored to its former Victorian glory. Now a cluster of exclusive boutiques it is a great shopping area, if slightly expensive.

Below

Mairangi Bay on the east coast of the North Auckland Peninsula is a popular beach and holiday resort. It looks out over the waters of the Hauraki Gulf to the extinct volcanic cone of Rangitoto Island.

Top left

Aucklanders are boat mad, there are said to be more private boats per family than second cars. There is a choice of sailing in all conditions within the many bays of the Waitemata Harbour and the vast Hauraki Gulf. The city's annual Anniversary Day Regatta is said to be the largest of its kind in the world.

Left

It was from an anchorage here in Mercury Bay that Captain Cook followed his "additional" voyage instructions of 1769 and hoisted the British flag on the 15th of November, claiming the land for King George III. Work on his primary task, to observe the Transit of Venus, enabling the calculating of the distance from the earth to the sun, was also continued from here.

Above

Whitianga Harbour is one of the most accessible on the Coromandel Coast. The town's full name "Whitianga-a-Kupe" refers to the legend of the polynesian explorer Kupe, who was said to have called here. Captain James Cook also gave a detailed description of a fortified pa on Whitianga Rock. Each summer this peaceful fishing town is invaded by fun seeking holidaymakers.

Below

Lottin Point is at the most northern tip of the North Island's East Cape. There are many magnificent seascapes along the East Cape road from Opotiki to Gisborne, where the golden sand and brilliant red of the flowering Pohutukawa contrast vividly with the green coastal grasslands which run right to the water's edge.

Right

Side by side with the pleasure craft of the inner harbour, Mount Maunganui is Tauranga's deep sea port which handles freight from the huge forest and paper pulp industry of the Bay of Plenty.

Far right

A typical camping area along the Bay of Plenty coastline. Here and right around the East Cape are scattered many sheltered bays, often privately owned and generously opened to the public by the local farmer in the holiday season.

Far right
Hamilton is the largest inland city in New Zealand and is the administration centre for some of the country's richest farmlands, the Waikato. The nearby Ruakura Research Centre enhances the importance of agriculture in the province.

Below
The town of Cambridge with its tree lined streets and village cricket green is very English in character, as is also the surrounding grasslands of the Waikato River where the English love of horses is evident in the many stud properties located on these lush pastures. Bloodstock from this district is eagerly sought after internationally.

Bottom
The rolling green hills of the King Country were once the independent territory of the much feared Maori King, Te Whiao. In those days it was forest covered but now is one of New Zealand's major sheep farming areas. The landscape however often reflects the rugged, formidable appearance of its early history.

Left

Pohutu Geyser, located in Whakarewarewa Maori Village in Rotorua is New Zealand's largest geyser. It has been known to play to heights of 31 metres and is sometimes active for hours at a time. Pohutu is one of Rotorua's major tourist attractions.

Bottom left

The heat created in these pools in Rotorua's geothermal area causes the mud to boil, creating fascinating patterns as air bubbles "plop" to the surface and the resulting shapes disappear in ever increasing circles.

Bottom right

The Waitomo Caves in the King Country attract visitors from all over the world. The three limestone caves open to the public display many long galleries of stalactites and stalagmites but are most famous for the "Glowworm Grotto", where visitors travel by boat along the subterranean river to view the silken threads of the larval grubs which shimmer in their thousands on the Grotto's ceiling.

Below

The harnessing of geothermal steam by the sinking of large bores and directing the gas into low pressure turbines is a phenomenon available to few countries. Here at Wairakei, world leading methods in geothermal power technology increase the amount of electricity available to New Zealand.

Left

Visitors to Rotorua pass through extensive forestry and sheep farming areas before the distinctive sulphur aroma announces that he or she has arrived at the very centre of New Zealand's geothermal area and the tourist and commercial centre of Maori arts and crafts, concerts and culture.

Above

Lake Okareka is found in the "hot lake" district and is only a short detour when travelling from Rotorua towards Lake Tarawera. It is one of many lakes in this area and although small in size makes up for it in beauty.

Below

Boating and fishing are the main holiday attractions at Lake Taupo and the bustling little town caters well for its annual influx of holidaymakers. There are ample motels, camping and caravan parks as well as luxurious fishing lodges nearby to cater for all tastes and pockets.

Right

The force of the 11 metre drop of water at the Huka Falls is increased greatly by the rapids immediately upstream where the fast flowing Waikato River narrows dramatically and surges over outcrops of rock shelves and rocky slides.

Far right

At Huka Village, a reconstructed town of days gone by, visitors can reflect on the living standards of the colonial days and the hours of toil required to keep the household and commercial facilities in working order.

30

Below
The symmetrical cone of Mt Ngauruhoe, 2,254 m, looks deceptively peaceful viewed here from the Whakapapanui Stream. It frequently can be seen belching steam and gas into the sky and more spasmodically ash and lava erupts spectacularly from its crater.

Right
New Zealand is blessed with an abundance of clear, clean, sparkling water. Throughout the land are to be found, lakes large and small, rivers wide and narrow and waterfalls dropping from huge heights or cascading through tiny bushclad drops like this one, the Matariki Falls on the Turangi National Park road.

Bottom right
This pastoral scene at the base of Mount Ruapehu is typical of the North Island of New Zealand, the development of rolling grassland as a result of the clearing and working of the dense bushland found beneath the volcanic peaks. Mt Ruapehu, the highest North Island mountain at 2,752 m is a major skiing resort in winter. The still active volcano's crater lake varies in temperature according to the thermal activity of the time, a useful warning device for geologists.

Above

Gisborne City is an important centre for the canning and processing of produce from the immense market gardening industry of the area. Historically also it is of significance as the place where the first Europeans, Capt. James Cook and his crew, landed on New Zealand soil on October 9th 1769. They made a hasty retreat however, after unfortunate Maori bloodshed and without their urgently required foodstuffs and water, thus the reason for Cook giving the name Poverty Bay to this piece of coastline.

Right

"As green and velvet-like as a well cared for golf course". The Waipukurau district, great sheep raising country in the Hawke's Bay, certainly fits this description.

Above

Lake Waikaremoana is generally regarded as the most beautiful in the North Island. It is located in the Urewera National Park, a vast area of ancient forest land. Keen trampers can walk right around the lake on a five day tramp through some of New Zealand's finest stands of rata, rimu and tawa, with a change to red then silver beech trees as you climb higher. The fishing and hunting here is said to be unequalled in the country.

Left

Farm buildings from colonial days are fascinating. They represent the centre from which New Zealand's agricultural strength grew, the stone and timber barns, woolsheds, stables and blacksmith's forge. Farmhands lived in slightly more comfortable quarters often with their own cookhouse like this one at Brancepeth in the Wairarapa. All reflect simple but efficient buildings to work in and from in the days when wool was clipped by hand and ploughs pulled by horses.

34

Below

Castlepoint near Masterton is a sheltered seaside resort on an otherwise inhospitable piece of coast, hence the Castlepoint lighthouse. A family resort with a long safe beach, it occasionally is the scene of an unusual race meeting where the number of your horse is decided after the bets have been placed.

Right

Napier is the largest city in Hawke's Bay, a major pastoral farming area in New Zealand, serviced by its own port. A severe earthquake in 1931 resulted in 256 deaths and the city in ruins but today there is little evidence of one of New Zealand's greatest catastrophes.

Bottom right

Pania of the Reef is a delightful little statue found on Napier's Marine Parade, an impressive esplanade lined with huge Norfolk Pines. Pania, legend tells us, was a sea person who was torn between her love for her human lover and her irresistible urge to return from whence she came.

Bottom left

Cape Kidnappers, reached by foot at lowtide along the beachfront from Clifton or by four wheel drive from Napier, is said to be the only mainland colony of Australian Gannets. Isolated islands are their preferred nesting grounds. The pairs live in very close proximity and over the summer months the noise of the thousands of parent birds and their chicks is unbelievable.

Top left

The port and city of New Plymouth have had a renewed input into their development and future in recent years. It has always flourished as the centre for export of cheese and secondary products from the rich dairy lands of Taranaki but the discovery of natural gas both on and offshore has led to much more investment, mainly foreign, which must benefit the region.

Bottom left

Pukearuhe was once the scene of much bloodshed in the days of the Maori Land Wars and uprising of the Hauhau movement. Located on an ancient Maori route between Taranaki and the Waikato, it is today a rich rural area, the soil well fertilized by early coverings of volcanic ash.

Above

In contrast to the massive mountain ranges of the South Island, Mount Egmont, recently reclaiming its Maori name of Taranaki, stands alone on the skyline. A dormant volcano with a symmetry reminiscent of Japan's Mt Fujiyama, Taranaki stands unrivalled in majesty amid the surrounding lush flora.

38

Below

Wanganui is one of New Zealand's oldest cities and is noted for its educational and cultural institution, The Sarjeant Art Gallery, which lives up to its reputation in both beauty of building and in its collection of early British and New Zealand paintings.

Right

Massey University in Palmerston North has for many years been the North Island's Agricultural College, specializing in research and allied studies. Today it also houses the country's Veterinary School.

Left

The rugged hill shapes and timber fence posts indicate Tatu's past as dense King Country bushland. In pockets still is found some of New Zealand's most picturesque native bush. European settlement came late to this and the neighbouring Taumarunui district on the headwaters of the Wanganui River, which adds to their present charm.

Below

The headwaters of the Wanganui River begin on the western side of the central volcanic mountains, cutting through narrow gorges and cascading over dozens of rapids through outstanding scenic country. For many years a canoeist's highway, it continues more sedately through Pipiriki and Jerusalem till it meets the sea at the city bearing its name, Wanganui.

Above

The Michael Fowler Centre designed by Sir Miles Warren has given Wellington an auditorium and concert venue of which it can be proud. Named after the then Mayor of Wellington, the centre has given the city's cultural life a real boost.

Right

In a few minutes commuters can be out of the office and walking to their Kelburn homes by way of Wellington's popular cable car which runs regularly from Lambton Quay to the top of the Botanical Gardens. In the early days of Wellington's development there was also a cable car here but drawn by horses.

Left

The addition of the "Beehive" to the existing old Parliament Building brought much controversy to Wellington from conservatives both local and throughout the country. Cartoonists and the media make good use of its unusual shape and its presence in the city adds renewed interest and dimensions to the centre of New Zealand's decision making.

Below

From Mount Victoria one can look right along Oriental Bay to downtown Wellington and through to the hill suburbs of the capital city. Built on a magnificent natural harbour, Wellington has an atmosphere of its own, exciting, progressive and without loss of character as often seen in larger sprawling cities.

THE SOUTH ISLAND

Only 22.5 kms of sea separates the South Island from the North but in this land of contrasts Cook Strait could seem to be separating two foreign countries, rather than islands. The differences are seen in the land and in its people.

The initial impact especially if arriving by air is the Southern Alps forming a backbone of snow covered peaks stretching nearly the length of the island. As the geothermal area of the north traces the fault-line from which New Zealand was formed, so do the mountains of the south. There are 27 major summits over 3,000 metres and 22 of them are found in the Mount Cook National Park. Another 130 throughout the island are over 2,400 metres in height.

This environment of mountains, lakes and forests is shared by South Islanders on both sides of the Alps. Climbers, skiers, trampers and holidaymakers all head to the high country for their weekend and holiday recreation. Perhaps Freud who said "I also visited New Zealand, but it was closed", should have "gone bush" also to see what makes New Zealanders, particularly South Islanders, the people they are. In the Southern Alps are found the three famous glaciers — the Franz Josef, Fox and Tasman. From Mt Cook village it is possible to fly by skiplane and land on the longest of the glaciers, the Tasman, then ski an uninterrupted 22 kms through the very heart of New Zealand's greatest mountains with Mount Cook "the cloud piercer", towering 3,705 metres above you.

The watershed of these mountains of the main divide form the spectacular lakes of the McKenzie Basin, Lake Tekapo with its turquoise glacial water, Pukaki where Mt Cook dominates the view at the head of the lake and the smaller Lake Ohau. In this grand highcountry tussockland are huge sheep stations which run from the peaks to the water's edge. Hardy merino sheep graze here and their fine wool is highly sort after by overseas buyers. A system of dams and canals from all three lakes join to form the Waitaki Hydro Electric Scheme with the earth dam at Benmore being one of the largest of its kind in the world.
Left
The Milford Track from Lake Te Anau to Milford Sound has been in use since 1888 and described as the "finest walk in the world". The Quinton Hut seen under the intimidating Mt Balloon, is a welcome sight for those having climbed out of the Clinton Valley and over the Mackinnon Pass, the hardest day on the 53 kilometre "walk".

The southern lakes of Hawea, Wanaka, Wakatipu, Hayes, Te Anau and Manapouri each have a beauty of their own, whether surrounded by bush, mountain ranges or peaceful farmlands as is Lake Hayes near the historic goldmining town of Arrowtown. Throughout Central Otago are relics and small towns such as St Bathans, recalling the goldrush days when the area was alive with prospectors and businessmen all with the same "get rich" dream associated with gold discoveries.

The east coast of the South Island is another area of contrasts. The Marlborough Sounds are the south's equivalent of the Bay of Islands. A yachtie's paradise, many of the bushclad coves and inlets are accessible only by boat. The temperate climate of the province is well suited to grape growing and hectares of vineyards give Marlborough a large share in New Zealand's rapidly expanding and improving wine industry.

Canterbury since its earliest settlement has been a farming province. Large sheep runs dominate the hill country while cropping and the growing of "Canterbury Lamb" is still the main output from the plains. The Canterbury plains are the largest area of flat land in the country, the monotony of which is broken only by the huge shingle riverbeds and lines of protective shelterbelts. The dominant wind of the plains is the mighty nor'west which can bring seasonal dust and drought or raging floods, as mountain storms send melted snow and rain in torrents down the province's many rivers. Further south the high rainfall in South Otago and inland Southland has its advantages for the farmers, who are seldom short of feed for the early fattening of stock.

The West Coast of the South Island, from Fiordland to Farewell Spit is a world apart. Separated from the rest of the island by the mountain barrier of the Southern Alps, it can only be reached by three passes, the Haast to the south and Arthur's and Lewis to the north. Its inaccessibility makes the deep fiords, Rimu forest and tiny bush girt lakes relatively unspoilt by man. In the far south the scenery of the Milford track is acclaimed worldwide but there are several lesser known walks of equal beauty. In places man has cleared the forest to allow dairy farming from bush to seashore, and as you travel north past the often storm swept Punakaiki Coast and the old coal mining towns of Westport and Karamea the landscape changes to subtropical with nikau palms giving the bush a jungle-like appearance.

Most South Island cities are really large towns serving the surrounding farming districts, apart from Christchurch the largest with a population of 322,000. There has been a steady population drift to the North Island over the recent years and Christchurch tries hard to compete with the larger North Island commercial companies. It has been claimed as being "more English than England", with its fine gothic cathedral, English styled private schools and central park reminiscent of London's Regent Park. Its elegant homes with their colourful gardens, tree lined avenues and fine old buildings on the banks of the Avon River, certainly remind one of "Mother England".

Dunedin on the other hand, is a replica of old Edinburgh. The city layout, street names and even the statues are the same. There are more hotels per head of population than anywhere in New Zealand, another Scottish tradition?

Many South Islanders prefer life with a slower pace, a more intimate community atmosphere — the pioneering West Coaster, the friendly Southland fisherman or Canterbury's descendants of the First Four ships. The South Island is a place of great natural beauty and allows a lifestyle for its people that blends harmoniously with it. That's the way they like it and for many the way they want to keep it.

Below
Totaranui, in the Abel Tasman National Park, is the beginning of an easy walkway through to the small township of Marahau. Along the track trampers pass many spectacular beaches with bush right to the shoreline. Birdlife is abundant, as are fish and molluscs. Goat Bay seen here with its golden sand and crystal clear water is one of the first passed along the two to three day walk.

Right
Kaiteriteri buzzes with activity at Christmas time. The holiday houses scattered amongst the surrounding hills are always full, as is the large motorcamp. However there are plenty of secluded neighbouring bays with idyllic views out to bush-clad islets for those who wish to retreat from the throngs of holidaymakers enjoying themselves in the clear blue water of the main beach.

Left

Abel Tasman in his ships Heemskerk and Zeehaen, sailed into Golden Bay just before Christmas of 1642. They were seeking fresh provisions and a well earned rest but received a hostile reception from the Maori warriors. Three sailors were slain and four more later died from wounds received. A memorial to Abel Tasman is to be seen here at Tata Beach, overlooking the twin Tata Islands where Tasman's sailors died.

Above

Broadgreen is one of several homes of
significant historic interest in Nelson.
Originally a cob house built in the style of a
Devonshire farmhouse in 1855, it has dainty
dormer windows and even a little children's
room. The whole interior is accurately and
elaborately decorated with chattels of its time.
Now in the care of the Historic Places Trust, it
will be enjoyed by many more generations of
New Zealanders.

Top right

It is the climate that attracts hundreds of
holidaymakers to Nelson's Tahunanui Beach.
The long sundrenched summers make it
attractive to the local folk to cool off after a
hard day in the nearby orchards or market-
gardens.

Right

On the section of the Inter-Island Ferry run
where Queen Charlotte Sound opens from
Cook Strait, and approaches its terminal at
Picton, passengers can see numerous holiday
houses nestled deep into the surrounding bush.
Families and friends arrive by winding road or
boat to enjoy the tranquillity, good fishing and
immense beauty of the Marlborough Sounds.

Left

The pear shaped Onawe Peninsula seen here in the Akaroa Harbour was a celebrated Maori fort in ancient times. In 1830 a horrible massacre took place when Te Rauparaha and his marauders from the north attacked members of the local Ngai-Tahu. Remaining earthworks of the defenders of Onawe are still to be found on the peninsula.

Below

The Maruia Falls were formed in 1929 during the devastating Murchison earthquake which lifted a section of road four metres. The path of the Maruia River was diverted to an area already upthrusted by previous earth movement, changing the landscape dramatically.

Bottom

The seaward Kaikoura Range at times looking as though it rises dramatically straight from the rugged coastline, makes a splendid backdrop for these gulls feeding at the Kahutara River mouth.

Top left

Christchurch deserves its reputation as a
Garden City, nowhere more so than in Hagley
Park. Here 500 acres in the city centre set aside
by the Founding Fathers for recreation, provide
ample sports facilities. Fine old English trees
and meandering paths follow the Avon River
past Rhododendrons, azalias, cherry blossoms,
and a carpet of daffodils in the spring.

Above

Cashmere, the hill suburb of Christchurch,
gives its residents a superb view over the city
and suburbs and further out to the plains and
magnificent peaks of the Southern Alps. Mt
Hutt, the well known commercial ski-field of
Canterbury is easily identified on a clear day.

Left

Cathedral Square has recently had a revamp
and is now a spacious area where inner city
workers may lunch and be entertained by
Christchurch's articulate Wizard, Bible Lady or
anyone else who wish to air their views.
Robert Godley, leader of the first city pilgrims,
stands watch over these modern happenings
with a stony expression.

Over

Canterbury is an important wool and lamb
producing area for New Zealand. The meat
fattened on the lush rolling hills and plains of
this province is exported to the EEC Countries,
Middle East, North America and Asia.

54

Right

Lake Tekapo in the McKenzie Country is renowned for its brilliant turquoise blue water, due to the fact that it is glacial fed via the Godley River. The lake covers an area of 83 sq kilometres and its rapidly expanding village is a popular base for skiing in the winter and trout fishing in the summer.

Below

From the Bealey Bridge on the Upper Waimakariri River mountaineers from Christchurch and much further afield can get a clear panorama of the Southern Alps. The road cut from Christchurch through the very spine of the alps and down to the goldfields of the West Coast, was explored and laid out by Arthur Dobson in 1865, hence the name for this climber's paradise, Arthur's Pass National Park.

Bottom

Having forced a passage through its spectacular gorge and down onto the wide Canterbury Plains, the web of the Waimakariri River meanders along the shingle riverbed to the sea. Centuries of such movement have built the plains into the fertile alluvial land it is today.

Below

A winter view of Lake Tekapo which is in the heart of an alpine basin. The altar of the tiny stone "Church of the Good Shepherd" is framed by a huge clear glass window, giving parishioners and its thousands of visitors a memorable view across the altar to the beauty of the lake and the Southern Alps.

Right

Lake Alexandrina's water is much clearer than the neighbouring Lake Tekapo, the difference being that it is rain-fed rather than glacier-fed. Alexandrina has a reputation shared with the adjoining Lake McGregor as being a fisherman's paradise and in the season keen anglers can be seen on both lakes casting from dinghy or shore.

Far right

One of the lesser known lakes in the McKenzie Country is Lake Middleton near Ohau, particularly attractive when the leaves of the surrounding trees are in their autumn colours.

58

Right

Surely the highlight of any trip to New Zealand would be to land on the Tasman Glacier in a ski plane and under the guides supervision, ski slowly down the snow covered 29 km of "frozen river", seeing for yourself the teal blue of the crevasses, listen to the roar of distant avalanches and gaze upwards to the soaring peaks which seem to envelope you in their majesty.

Below

Mt Cook, easily identified by its twin peaks, is New Zealand's highest mountain at 3764 m. Called "Aorangi" or the "cloud piercer" by the Maori, it stands 300 m above any of the surrounding peaks. Mountaineers worldwide are attracted to challenge its massive summit, often hidden by forbidding clouds as a result of the fierce north-west wind prevalent in the Main Divide. It is a mountain to be approached only with the respect it is due.

Far left

The peaceful appearance of the head of Lake Benmore belies its busy role as the site of the largest single power producing station in the Southern Hemisphere when it was constructed. The curving earth dam on the Waitaki River contains 28 million ton of material and has created this manmade lake, a resort area for boating and angling.

Above

Wanaka has wide appeal as a holiday resort all year round since the establishment of Treble Cone and Cardrona ski-fields in the area. Many believe its lake to be the most beautiful in the country. The surrounding landscape is more gently contoured than that of Hawea or Wakatipu and the curving shoreline, especially here at Glendhu Bay, lends itself to summer swimming and camping.

Left

On leaving Christchurch for the West Coast the first mountains reached are the Torlesse Range with magnificent views down to the plains of the Waimakariri riverbed, or westward to the Craigieburns, the location for several of Canterbury's ski-fields. Brooksdale Station in the foreground is one of several sheep runs on the road to Arthur's Pass.

Above

The waters of Lake Wanaka are often calm and reflect the surrounding hills and mountains of the Mount Aspiring National Park. Accessible by car via the Matukituki Valley, the sight of Mt Aspiring rising dramatically out of the alpine scenery is well worth the half day drive.

Right

A visit to Arrowtown is like walking back in time. Though principally a tourist centre, the original wooden and stone dwellings along the tiny main street and scattered throughout the little township look like and are lived in as in the days when the town was a thriving gold settlement. This has been achieved by skilful town planning and a visit to the Arrowtown Museum, part of which dates back to 1875, tells many a tale of days gone by.

Above

Named Te Wai Whaka-ata, "the waters of reflection" by the ancient Maori, Lake Hayes is a favourite area for artists and photographers. The rural setting makes its beauty peaceful in its appeal.

Top right

The mighty Clutha River, seen here near Luggate, rises at Lake Wanaka and winds past the orchards of Cromwell, Alexandra and Roxburgh, meeting the Pacific Ocean below Balclutha. It carries the largest volume of water of any river in New Zealand, while a second major dam to the one at Roxburgh, being constructed at Clyde, will increase its kilowatt output even more. Unfortunately parts of the historic and scenically superb Cromwell Gorge and its old township will be flooded in the name of progress.

Right

The road to Skippers through the Shotover Gorge near Queenstown is intimidating to most drivers. It winds and twists through breathtaking rugged landscape, with towering rock formations, derelict buildings from early mining days and gravel banks of dredge trailings. Across the Skippers Bridge, 90 metres above the Shotover River, is the site of the old town where thousands toiled and died in the search for gold.

Left

The resort of Queenstown, the heart of the South Island's tourist industry, can be enjoyed to the full from the Skyline lookout, reached by Gondola. From here the panorama of the near perfect S shaped Lake Wakatipu and The Remarkables range provide the township with a location comparable to any of its kind in the world.

Below

An enjoyable excursion from Queenstown is to take the old steam ferry affectionately known as the "Lady of the Lake", to Walter Peak Station situated under the mountain of the same name seen here on the other side of the lake. When the service began in 1912 passengers on the T.S.S. Earnslaw had to share the ride with sheep and supplies for any of the runs enroute.

Above

The end is almost in sight on the Routeburn track, following the falls past the National Park Board's huts down to the grassy flats and on to Queenstown. This national walkway includes a variety of beech forest and alpine lakes, tussockland and rock country before dropping dramatically to the Routeburn Valley below.

Top right

The 39 km Routeburn track through remote and varied New Zealand backcountry is a favourite with trampers, linking the two main tourist centres of Queenstown and Milford by way of an old Maori greenstone trail. Lake Harris, near the summit is a popular resting place on this reasonably easy walk. Good bus access is available at both ends of the track and the hut facilities are excellent.

Right

From the township of Glenorchy at the head of Lake Wakatipu trampers can head into the valleys of the Rees and Dart Rivers, gems for those who enjoy the backcountry without the crowds of the more commercial tracks. The Glenorchy Races at New Year, when horses from surrounding stations contest events unheard of by the racing fraternity, is a real New Zealand experience.

Above

Lake Gunn on the Te Anau – Milford Road, is an angler's paradise plentiful with brown and rainbow trout. Along with Lake Fergus, it is the source of the Eglinton River.

Right

The Sutherland Falls, reached on foot by the Milford Track, are recorded as being the fourth highest in the world. When Lake Quill above the falls is in flood, the water cascades down some 580 m in one single leap, an impressive sight by anyone's standards.

Far right

Mitre Peak — 1722 m, can best be appreciated on the deep fiord of Milford Sound, where one can clearly see the bush approach and difficult rock faces. One of the largest mountains in the world rising straight from the sea, its photograph is widely used in brochures enticing tourists to New Zealand.

Above

The path leading to Lake Matheson begins just outside Fox township. It is a chance to stroll through the Rimus, Kahikatea and many ferns of the native bush and listen to the songs of the Tui, Bellbirds and Fantails which follow inquisitively. The sight of the mirror-like lake framed by some of the highest peaks of the Southern Alps is an added bonus.

Right

The road leading to Franz Josef Glacier winds through typical Westcoast rain forest before opening onto the terminal moraine of the glacier. Along the side of the road several short tracks lead to local beauty spots.

Left

Maori legend tells us that Franz Josef Glacier was formed by the tears of Hine on discovering her beloved Wawa had fallen to his death from a precipice below her. The tears turned to a river of ice as a memorial. Recent records show the glacier is increasing in length again, a real boost for the local tourist industry.

Below

The pancake rocks at Punakaiki, 56 km from Westport, are an interesting sight. They are formed by the action of heavy seas and rainfall on the limestone rock where the softer surface erodes leaving only the harder slabs. On a stormy day huge blowholes send roaring jets of water skyward.

Above

Timaru's manmade harbour offers shelter to coastal vessels that sail these exposed waters. Nearby, for three weeks of the Christmas Holidays, the beach and gardens of Caroline Bay are the scene of a summer festival when musicians, sideshows, ferriswheel and bathing beauties entertain the crowds.

Top right

Oamaru is a fine well planned centre for North Otago's farming district. Its attractive layout and white stone buildings give it a handsome dignity. Oamaru stone when first quarried can be cut by a carpenter's saw, but when left to the air it hardens. When used in a clear-aired sea town such as Oamaru it retains its distinctive creamy white colour for years.

Right

The Moeraki ("Potato") boulders, Maori legend tells us, are the result of the capsizing of the canoe Arai-te-Uru from the legendary Maori homeland of Hawaiki. The wreck and its precious cargo, gourds of kumara (sweet potato) seed, were washed ashore here and turned to stone. The huge boulders of septarian stone are scattered all along this piece of Otago coastline.

Above

The city of Dunedin was once the most prosperous in New Zealand. During and after the Otago Gold Rush in 1861, it was the commercial centre where many an entrepreneur made his fortune from the goldfields. From the sea suburb of St Clair one can see across low lying south Dunedin to the city, harbour and Signal Hill.

Right

Larnach Castle on the Otago Peninsula has had a chequered existence. Built about 1880 by the Hon. W. J. M. Larnarch as a residence befitting his wife's station in life as daughter of the Pretender to the French throne, no expense was spared. It is full of wonders, the rare mottled kauri carved stair handrail, hand embossed venetian glass in the entrance and a magnificent ballroom where one previous tenant wintered his sheep.

Far right

As well as its distinctly Victorian character, strong Scottish history and proud reputation as a University town, Dunedin can also boast of its great location. Viewing the city and harbour from the northern motorway makes one of the most impressive city approaches in New Zealand.

Left

The fertile Southland farms are renowned for the number of sheep they can successfully carry per acre. Fortrose, once an early whaling station, is on Southland's exposed eastern coastline but even here the fat lambs are very impressive.

Below

The Waiau river pictured here near Tuatapere begins at Lake Te Anau and flows through the rich farm land of western Southland. It reaches the sea at Blue Cliffs, one of the few beaches where the New Zealand shellfish delicacy "Toheroa" can be found.

Bottom

The Dunedin City Council has its own electricity grid fed by the artificial lake at Mahinerangi. The surrounding exotic forests also provide an income for this forward thinking Council.

Above

Port Pegasus, Stewart Island, is visited only by
fishermen and very determined trampers.
Once a small mining centre it has now reverted
to its natural state where seals and sea
elephant can occasionally bask in the not too
warm sun, their stomachs full of fish so prolific
in these waters.

Left

Bluff harbour near Invercargill is famous for
its fleet of fishing boats which work the prolific
waters of Foveaux Strait and the western
coastline. Fish, crays and oysters are the catch
and descendants of the Rakiura tribe also have
the right to trap the thousands of Muttonbirds
that flock annually to the islands in these
waters.

First published in paperback in 1986
This edition published 1989 reprinted 1990, 1992
by Kowhai Publishing Ltd
299 Moorhouse Avenue, Christchurch
10 Peacock Street, Auckland

Photographs copyright © Warren Jacobs
Photography Ltd
Christchurch

Designed and typeset in New Zealand
Printed in Hong Kong
ISBN 0 908598–38–6